# HOW TO FEEL GOOD
# ABOUT YOURSELF

Bryan E. Robinson, Ph.D.
Jamey McCullers, R.N.

Health Communications, Inc.
Deerfield Beach, Florida

Publisher: Health Communications, Inc.
3201 S.W. 15th Street
Deerfield Beach, FL 33442-8190

Graphic design by Graphic Expression
Color design by Robert Cannata

# How To Feel Good About Yourself

If someone asked us to make a list of all our character faults, we could easily make a long list. It is so easy to see our shortcomings, yet very hard to see our strengths. We have been shown and told of our drawbacks for so long that they stand out above all else.

These *Healograms* — positive, healthy messages we send to ourselves — help us feel good about ourselves. They help us to see both sides of the coin — the pluses and minuses — and to love ourselves, along with our imperfections. *Healograms* show us how to empower ourselves and how to restore good feelings, joy and balance in our lives. Write your own *Healograms* in the spaces provided.

These affirming messages remind us that life is full of ups and downs. There are bad times and good times. We get hired and fired. We get recognized and overlooked, loved and rejected, given credit and blamed. Sometimes we feel great and other times small. *Healograms* keep us strapped in for life's roller coaster ride. They help us realize we cannot change the ups and downs of life but we can adjust our inner selves. If you want to stay steady and secure and to continue to feel good about yourself during life's ups and downs, these *Healograms* are for you.

# How To Feel Good About Yourself

# Overcoming Self-Doubt

Self-doubt is one of those cruel ghosts that can haunt us day and night. Can we still perform? Are we still lovable? Self-doubt goes ahead of us like a scouting party before we face challenging situations. It stalks us when we have a big day on the job and lurks over our shoulders when we're trying to make our relationships work. It reminds us we don't have forever to complete our tasks on this planet.

Everybody has self-doubt now and then. Doubt is an old tape from the past that replays in the present. Acknowledging and accepting doubtful thoughts, rather than pretending they don't exist, gives us power over them. We discover how to live with self-doubt without letting it paralyze us. When we believe in ourselves and persist in our efforts, self-doubt loses its power over us. We are in charge of it. It is not in charge of us. We move forward. We participate in life.

*Self-doubt cannot keep us from taking the risks that we need for our personal growth as long as we face ourselves honestly and accept ourselves totally.*

# Getting Along With Ourselves

Many of us want to be someplace that we are not. When we're at home, we want to be at the beach. At the beach we long to be back in our own beds again. We seek distant lands in search of happiness and when we don't find it there, we look elsewhere.

An unhappy starfish who lived in the ocean asked the wise old whale where he could find the sea. The whale answered, "It's all around you." The frustrated starfish replied, "This is just the ocean; I'm looking for the sea," and swam away continuing his search.

This type of restlessness comes from an empty relationship with ourselves. We busy ourselves looking for something or someone to make us happy when it's already here. We are where we belong. Getting along with ourselves will take us on adventures we never dreamed possible.

We can eliminate endless searching and restlessness and live the life we want as long as we learn to get along with ourselves.

# Being Your Own Best Friend

People give us the same respect we give ourselves. If we put ourselves down or minimize our worth, others will too.

We have been taught that self-sacrifice is a great virtue. But always putting ourselves last is just as detrimental as always putting ourselves first. We teach others how to treat us by the way we treat ourselves. We can ask our-

9

selves, "Am I kind to myself?" or "Do I treat myself as I would like to be treated by others?" The way we want to be treated must first come from us, not from someone else.

As we nurture and respect ourselves, we show others how we expect them to treat us. We do not settle for second best because we are truly our own best friend.

We teach others how to treat us by the way we treat ourselves. As we nurture and respect ourselves, we show others how we expect them to treat us.

# 4

# Working On Ourselves

Many of us are experts at evaluating and judging others because it keeps the spotlight off ourselves. The fact is that the defects we point out in others are the very things we don't like about ourselves. So if we want to know what improvements we can make in ourselves, all we have to do is notice the things for which we condemn others.

Instead of taking other people's inventory, we can begin to take our own. Next time we feel the urge to assassinate someone else's character, we can turn the spotlight inward and examine ourselves. Whatever it is about them we don't like is a reflection of something we don't like in ourselves. If someone is too slow, we may feel deep down that we are not moving fast enough in our own lives. Our complaints, judgments and criticisms are sources of information that tell us what we need to work on within ourselves.

*Our complaints, judgments and criticisms are sources of information that tell us what we need to work on within ourselves.*

# 5

# Feeling Good About Ourselves

Confucious once said, "The grass must bend when the wind blows over it." When we look at the relationship between wind and grass, we can ask ourselves if we are in relationships where we're always the grass, blown about by the wants and whims of others. Do we feel as if we're always underfoot?

As long as we feel unequal to others, it's hard to act equally in relationships with them. We have a choice. We don't have to make ourselves inferior to others. We can care and love ourselves so that we are on an equal plane with loved ones, colleagues and friends. Once we begin to love and care for ourselves, others will love and care for us too. As we learn to blow with the wind, we treat ourselves with equality, not inferiority.

*As* we begin to love and care for ourselves, others will love and care for us too.

# 6

# Loving Ourselves

Sometimes we spend so much time beating ourselves up that we don't have time for others. Or we get so wrapped up in taking care of ourselves that we forget about the needs of others.

Our goal is self-love, that midpoint somewhere between self-contempt and self-centeredness. We cannot love and be loved by others if we cannot love ourselves, then get beyond ourselves. When we love ourselves first, we have more to give away and we can give and receive it freely. When we move to the middle of the line between self-contempt and self-centeredness, our needs are met but not at the expense of others. As we learn to take care of ourselves without getting wrapped up in ourselves, we discover that there is always time to love and care for others.

*Once* we can love ourselves without becoming self-centered, we have more to give away and we can give and receive love freely.

# 7

# Building Confidence

Crutches are used to support those who cannot walk. What crutches do we use to keep our spirits up? Alcohol? Food? Relationships? Sex? All of the above? We are spiritually disabled as long as we depend on our addictive crutches to get us through the day. We toddle or hobble, but we never walk on our own confidence.

Spiritual healing helps us throw down our addictive crutches and walk on our own with strength from our Higher Power, a strength that sustains us no matter how difficult the pace. We trade in the crutches for something far more substantial — a greater understanding of the universe, ourselves and our relationship to life. We work through each day, one by one and step by step. We outgrow our crutches as children outgrow their clothes and develop healthier lives that fit better with the new person we have become.

$W$e build in confidence when we outgrow our emotional crutches as children outgrow their clothes and develop healthier lives that fit better with
the new person we have become.

# 8

# Overcoming Self-Righteousness

Do we think we know all the answers now that we have started our spiritual journey? Do we silently judge others because they are not on the same path? Do we believe we are always right and others wrong?

Our smugness is just another form of silent judgment. It is a way of letting perfectionistic attitudes of always being right creep into our personalities. Always being right is a burden we no longer need in our personal development. We can only know what is best for ourselves, not for anyone else. We can never know another's heart or what their inner needs are. We have not been appointed anyone's judge or jury.

We can accept others, who do not live their lives as we do, as being exactly where they need to be. We can put our energies into improving our lives to the best of our ability and leave others to take care of their own.

We can take our self-righteous attitudes and put them to good use on ourselves by accepting others who do not live their lives as we do and knowing they are exactly where they need to be.

# 9

# Honoring The
# Beauty Within

Many of us have been taught
that we must have some physical
attraction to have beauty. But
how often do we stop to look at
the beauty that lies within us?

Each of us has our own inner
beauty that needs no adornment
or external adjustment. This is
our source of lasting and true
happiness. That inner part of us
is there waiting to be discovered

and to radiate outward. By silently meditating, we can go to that core being within where we can discover our own beauty.

We may have been taught that it is selfish to focus upon ourselves. But others learn to treat us by how they see us perceiving ourselves. When we see the beauty and good in ourselves, others will see it also and we will see it in them. Treating ourselves with love and honor teaches others to treat us with mutual love and honor.

*Each of us has our own inner beauty that needs no adornment or external adjustment. This is the source of lasting and true happiness.*

# 10

# Learning From Our Mistakes

Josh Billings once said, "It ain't no disgrace for a man to fall, but to lie there and grunt is." Life is full of its ups and downs. There are times when all of us fall down. We forget, make errors or say or do the wrong thing. But no matter how serious the fall, we don't have to wallow in self-pity. We can get up, brush ourselves off and keep on keeping on.

We can look at our mistakes as lessons and always ask what we have learned. But we never have to give up or condemn ourselves with shame and guilt. There will be more bumps and spills on life's journey. That's just the way it is. We can use these lessons to strengthen ourselves so that we will be stronger for the next lesson. Today we did the best we could; tomorrow we will be stronger.

*Our mistakes can teach us much and make us strong as long as we use them as lessons to strengthen ourselves so that we will be stronger for the next lesson.*

## Feeling Comfortable
## In Our Own Skins

Are we comfortable in our own skins? Or are we always wishing we were someone else? When we cannot find contentment in ourselves, it is useless to seek it elsewhere. Many of us are always telling ourselves that if certain conditions existed, that would change how we feel inside. But that's not how the world works.

When we try to find happiness by searching for it, we will find it, as the old woman did her lost spectacles, safe on her own nose all the time. No matter where we go or what happens to us, the outer conditions do not change our inner conditions. It's the other way around. Our inner thoughts and feelings change the outer conditions of our lives. We live inside ourselves and can never escape ourselves. The remedies for self-lack and the ills of the soul are found by looking within and learning to feel comfortable in our own skins.

*The* remedies for self-lack and the ills of the soul are found by looking within and learning to feel comfortable in our own skins.

# Completing
# The Past

To get the best out of our lives now, it is important to complete the past by tying up loose ends: broken relationships, unkept promises, unresolved misunderstandings, a task put off for too long.

One approach to resolving past incompletions is to make a list of all persons with whom we have unfinished business or whom we have harmed in any way and to make amends to them all.

By making amends we shed long-held feelings, clear the air of misunderstanding and give finality to the cloud of incompletion that darkened our lives. Once we have tied up loose ends, we can deal with new challenges instead of letting them stockpile and clutter our minds. This gives us more energy for living life in the present.

*O*nce we have tied up loose ends, we are better prepared to deal with new challenges one at a time, instead of letting them stockpile and clutter our minds.

# 13

# Getting Connected

Many of us are successful in what we do and have all the material comforts of life. But why do we feel so unhappy and lonely as if something is missing? When we feel empty, our natural inclination is to fill the hole with something, such as food, buying things, work or alcohol. Too few of us are plugged into a spiritual connection. We go from one relationship to another or from job to job, trying to connect but still feeling unconnected.

Once we make spiritual contact within ourselves, the hole is filled and we begin to feel complete and connected. We feel plugged into life just as a light bulb is connected to an electrical current. Once connected, we let the same life force that makes trees grow take charge of our lives and shine through us.

*We can make spiritual contact within ourselves and feel plugged into life just as a light bulb is connected to an electrical current.*

# 14

# Making A Humility Check

Sometimes we trick ourselves into thinking that acquiring power and building an image brings us self-fulfillment and that we are above the laws and rules of society. When haughty thinking strikes, it's time for a humility check.

Humility is about being ourselves — not some image we try to project. It's about seeing ourselves as we truly are and learning to be genuine with others. Once we can feel comfortable with who we are, without clouds of self-importance or worthlessness, we have learned humility.

We move through our lives without pretense and false pride and without self-neglect and self-inadequacy. We are just ourselves, no more and no less. We vow to be ourselves and let the real part of us shine through in all our daily interactions.

*When* we can feel comfortable with who we are, without clouds of self-importance or worthlessness, we have learned humility . . . to just be ourselves and nothing more or less.

# Making Up Our Minds To Be Happy

Abraham Lincoln once said, "Most folks are as happy as they make up their minds to be." But many of us respond to that saying with, "How can I be happy when I have so much strife at work and disharmony at home?"

We can make up our minds to be happy or unhappy, regardless of the circumstances. We can decide to give happiness equal time with despair. The dualities of joy and sadness, hate and love, right and wrong, good and evil are part of life's total package.

By making up our minds to feel joy, happiness, love and good, we treat ourselves to a more balanced experience of life. Of course there will be tough times. But we can give the positive influences in life equal time by concentrating on optimism instead of pessimism, by making up our minds to be happy.

*By* making up our minds to feel joy, happiness, love and good, we treat ourselves to a more balanced, self-satisfying experience of life.

# Healograms In This Series
## Series 3

1. How To Feel Good About Yourself
2. How To Reduce Your Stress
3. How To Get The Best Out Of Life
4. How To Have A Healthy Outlook

# Healograms
## Series 1

1. How To Take Care Of Yourself
2. How To Live Your Life To The Fullest

3. How To Resolve The Conflict In Your Life
4. How To Make Your Life A Miracle

## Healograms
## Series 2

1. How To Feel Good In Relationships
2. How To Learn To Love Yourself
3. How To Boost Your Self-Esteem
4. How To Heal Your Inner Child

---

To order, call: 1-800-851-9100